P is for Piñata

A Mexico Alphabet

Written by Tony Johnston and Illustrated by John Parra

for Carlos Stephens, Salvador Villar, and my Mexican cuates

TONY

for my parents, Del and Cecilia, for their love and support, through all my years

JOHN

Sleeping Bear Press®
310 North Main Street, Suite 300
Chelsea, MI 48118
www.sleepingbearpress.com

© 2008 Sleeping Bear Press is an imprint of Gale, a part of Cengage Learning.

Printed and bound in Canada.

First Edition

10 9 8 7 6 5 4 3 2 1

Library of Congress Cataloging-in-Publication Data

Johnston, Tony, date.
P is for piñata : a Mexico alphabet / written by Tony Johnston ;
illustrated by John Parra.
p. cm.
Summary: "Using the alphabet, Mexico is introduced in this picture
book using poetry and detailed expository text. A through Z topics include:
adobe, Diego Rivera, Lady of Guadalupe, lava, prickly pear, and skeleton"—
Provided by publisher.

ISBN 978-1-58536-144-1

1. Mexico—Juvenile literature. 2. Alphabet books—Juvenile literature.
I. Parra, John, ill. II. Title.
F1208.5.J64 2008
972—dc22   2008024804

Mexico

In Mexico, adobe mud has been used since the earliest times to build houses. Workers combine mud and straw and mix it with their bare feet. It is squishy work! They fill wooden molds called *adoberas* with the mud mixture, let them dry in the sun, then carefully tap out the bricks.

Adobe is a good material for a house. It keeps rooms cool in summer and comfortable in winter. But sometimes it shakes down in earthquakes.

Houses are still built with adobe bricks, not only in Mexico, but around the world. Because of the handwork (and footwork) to make it, in some countries like the United States, adobe costs a lot.

Once in a while when adobe bricks are sunning, a dog or cat or turkey steps through the wet mud. The tracks dry there and, when the house is built, become part of a wall or floor. When you see them, they are a kind of greeting from a small creature.

A is for Adobe

Adobe is a certain kind of brick.
It's made from straw and mud that's very thick.

B is for Ballet Folklórico

Oh, hear the lively music!
Oh, see the nimble feet prance!
Oh, feel the beat of Mexico!
Oh, dance, dance, DANCE!

The Ballet Folklórico de México (Folk Ballet of Mexico) is the dream of Amalia Hernández. When she was eight she told her father, "I want to learn to dance." Amalia learned how to dance, and how to create patterns of dance—choreography. She learned that what made her happiest were the music and dances from her own country.

In 1952 she began a dance company that traveled to Cuba, Canada, and later to California, performing in a colorful explosion of dance that perfectly represented Mexico— her creative energy, her history. After years of work, and triumph at Chicago's Pan-American Games, President López Mateos supported Amalia to create "one of the best ballets in the world." And she did. With a troupe of over fifty, the Ballet Folklórico gained world renown.

If you are lucky enough to see a performance, try to see it in Mexico City, at the Palace of Fine Arts. The Tiffany glass curtain, with its purple volcanoes, the snowy Ixta and Popo, sets the tone for what is to come. The curtain vanishes; the music begins. Your feet can't stop tapping. Your whole body moves in your seat. The music, the colors, the beauty of movement, the energy—the whole marvelous spectacle—will take your breath away. You are seeing a woman's life work—and a little girl's dream.

Mexico is the "birthplace" of cacao, the plant that gives us chocolate. Its scientific name, *Theobroma cacao*, means "food of the gods." Chocolate lovers must think that's the perfect name. Since long before the Spanish invasion, the Olmecs (1500–400 BC) on the Gulf Coast drank a beverage made from cacao.

Cacao beans were highly prized in the Americas. They were used for money and hauled by traders in bulky backpacks over far-flung trade routes. Prices from 1545 list a tomato as worth one cacao bean; a male turkey at two hundred. Only the noblest classes drank chocolate, a holy potion, the foamier the better. The Aztecs came up with the first known word for chocolate, *cacahuatl* (cacao water); the finest was called *tlaquetzalli*, precious thing. So precious was chocolate, royalty drank it from special cups and only in sacred rituals. Poets wrote about it.

The Aztec's drink was cold and bitter; mixed with flowers, corn, even chilies. In 1575 one European writer called it "a strange, murky, sinister-looking beverage."

Columbus brought the first chocolate "seeds" to Europe. Spaniards had incredible sweet tooths, so they came up with a sweet, hot chocolate, which became the rage. (It was also a great disguise for poison, a popular way to do your enemies in!) Eventually, cacahuatl took on a solid form—candy.

C is for Cacao

Chocolate! Oh, chocolate!
We drink it hot or cold.
The beans were prized by Aztec kings
and worth as much as gold.

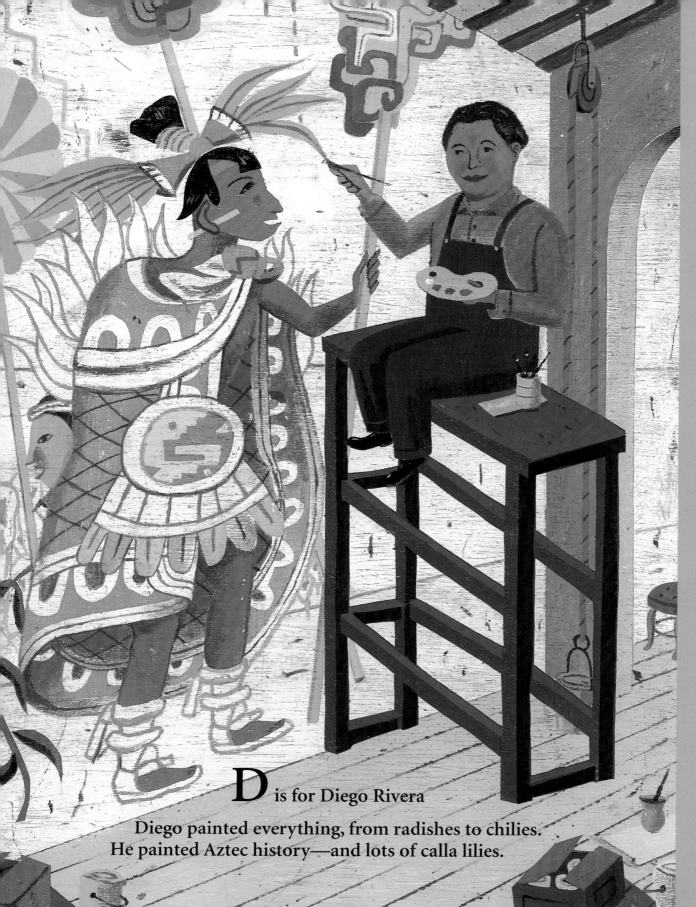

D is for Diego Rivera

Diego painted everything, from radishes to chilies.
He painted Aztec history—and lots of calla lilies.

Diego Rivera was a painter who was best known as one of the three great Mexican muralists (artists who paint on walls). The others were José Clemente Orozco and David Alfaro Siquieros. Many of Diego's works have political themes. Murals for the courtyard of the National Palace show the destruction of the high Aztec civilization by the brutish Cortés and his Spanish invaders.

In New York's Rockefeller Center, in 1933, Rivera began a mural that included a portrait of the Russian leader Lenin, whose ideas went against Mr. Rockefeller's. When Rockefeller had the unfinished work painted over, Diego re-created it in the Palace of Fine Arts in Mexico City.

Diego was married to Frida Kahlo and lived with her in the Casa Azul (Blue House). He jokingly called himself her "frog prince" because he thought he looked like a gigantic frog.

Diego Rivera was devoted to the Mexican people. During his lifetime, he built a dark, brooding private temple named Anahuacalli (house near water). He filled it with his personal collection of pre-Cortés art, many artworks he had created, and a model of his studio. When he died, he gave Anahuacalli to his Mexicans as a museum. It is a place for them to go and to remember their marvelous heritage.

Dd

E is for Emperor

Some of Mexico's emperors
died quite suddenly.
Truth is, to be emperor there
was not very healthy.

Maximilian I

In Aztec days there were emperors. The last, Moctezuma II, was killed by the Spaniards during the conquest of Mexico. Centuries later, the idea came up again and Augustín Iturbide became emperor, briefly.

In the 1850s liberals and conservatives fought a lot. Finally Benito Juárez, a liberal, became president. Some rich Mexicans wanted property given back to large land-owners (themselves); property that Juárez had taken. They schemed to import an emperor and overthrow him. The United States was too busy with its Civil War to stop it. So, with Napoleon III of France and French troops supporting him, Maximilian von Hapsburg, Archduke of Austria, crossed the Atlantic Ocean in 1864 to rule Mexico.

Although Maximilian made laws to help "his people," canceling debts of over ten pesos for peasants and stopping child labor, he was more like a storybook ruler. He spent a lot of money beautifying Chapultepec Castle, where he and his empress lived. He built the grand avenue, Paseo de la Emperatríz (now Reforma) so that after outings in their Cinderella-like carriage, they could be dropped off at their front door.

Most Mexicans didn't welcome Maximillian. His followers were mostly cooks, guards, gardeners, and be-medaled generals. When the Civil War ended, Americans focused on tossing the French out of Mexico. Maximilian was captured in 1867 by Juárez's soldiers and shot by a firing squad. His "empire" fizzled out.

Ff

The variety of Mexican folk art is astonishing. Items of charm, humor, and beauty are created out of just about anything. You can find "paintings" made from yarn; bread-dough figures; tin tree ornaments; bands of straw musicians; cornhusk dolls; fantastic wooden creatures; intricately carved gourds; enormous devils and angels of papier-mâché. If you search you may even find a colorful Lady of Guadalupe made from the pod of a tree!

And there are countless clay items—from skull magnets to flamboyant trees of life to flowerpot mermaids, holding combs for their flowing hair.

Victor Fosado of Oxaca helped make people aware of the energy and grace of folk art, as did the painter Chucho Reyes. Maestro Gorky Gonzales Quiñones, a potter from Guanajuato, is renowned. Because his work is of such high quality and because, apart from original pieces, he re-creates historical designs, Gorky is considered a national treasure.

There is no end to Mexican creativity!

F is for Folk Art

Gourds to seeds to colored string,
there is art in everything!

Gg

G is for Lady of Guadalupe

The Lady of Guadalupe
is the saint of Mexico.
One winter, in the freezing ground,
she made red roses grow.

The Lady of Guadalupe is Mary, the mother of Jesus. According to Mexican legend, on December 9, 1531, the blessed Lady appeared to Juan Diego, a poor Aztec Indian once known as He-who-speaks-like-an-eagle. The Lady wanted a church to be built there, on the hill of Tepeyac, a church for everybody, especially the Indians. Nobody believed that the Lady had sent Juan Diego to ask such a favor, let alone that he had seen her. So she sent proof—roses in winter, roses where none had ever grown. Juan Diego filled his *tilma* (cloak of cactus fiber) with the blooms. When he poured them out to show scoffers, a picture of the Lady remained on the cloth. Because of this miracle, the Lady of Guadalupe became the patron saint of Mexico and the Americas.

The church of the Lady of Guadalupe stands where Juan Diego once saw her. What remains of the tilma is displayed there still. Each year millions of faithful pilgrims make their way from the farthest, smallest villages throughout the country to see the holy cloth and pay homage to their saint.

H is for Hairless Dog

The hairless is not bird, nor fish, nor frog.
It could be called the very first hot dog.

The Mexican hairless dog, *tepeizeuintli*, *xoloitzcuintli*, or *esquincle* for short, is completely naked except for an occasional bit of head fuzz. Some people might call this dog hideous, but to an esquincle lover, it is *hermosísimo*, gorgeous.

This dog is ancient. And its body temperature is warmer than other dogs'. Because of this, in Aztec times these critters were used as bed warmers. You could say they were America's first hot dogs! Pre-Cortés pottery from the state of Colima shows them in a variety of poses. One particularly charming hollow pot is shaped like a dog with one flat side, to be filled and used as a hot water bottle. In early times, as now, the Mexicans had a wonderful sense of humor!

Though small, the lively breed makes excellent watchdogs. In olden Mexico, hairless dogs were also used to lick a person's body clean—and as food. Though they are rare, esquincles live on today. These dogs are just as hideous—or gorgeous—as they ever were. And they are just as hot. But they are no longer eaten for dinner. They are beloved and pampered pets.

H h

is for Independence Monument

Mexico's Independence Day
is the sixteenth of September.
The people built a monument
to remember, to remember.

Ii

The monument to Mexican Independence stands one hundred fifty feet tall, in the middle of the Reforma, the avenue that ribbons its way through the heart of Mexico City. The soaring pillar was designed by Antonio Rivas Mercado. Work on it began in 1901 and took nine years to complete.

El Angel, as the monument is fondly called, is crowned with a gold-gilded bronze figure, cast in Florence, Italy. The base in adorned with statues of heroes of the Independence: Guerrero, Mina, Bravo, Hidalgo. On September 15, 1810, Father Hidalgo gave *El Grito*, the famous shout that began the fight for independence: *¡Méxicanos, viva México!* Mexicans, long live Mexico! Independence is celebrated on September 16, but each year at eleven o'clock on the night before, in every town square *El Grito* echoes again.

In 1957, the column, angel and all, came tumbling down in an earthquake and was rebuilt. From the "aerie" near the top, you get a very "WOW!" view of the city—except when it's too smoggy.

Mexicans look at the Independence Monument with pride. Maybe when they see it they shout inside *¡Méxicanos, viva México!*

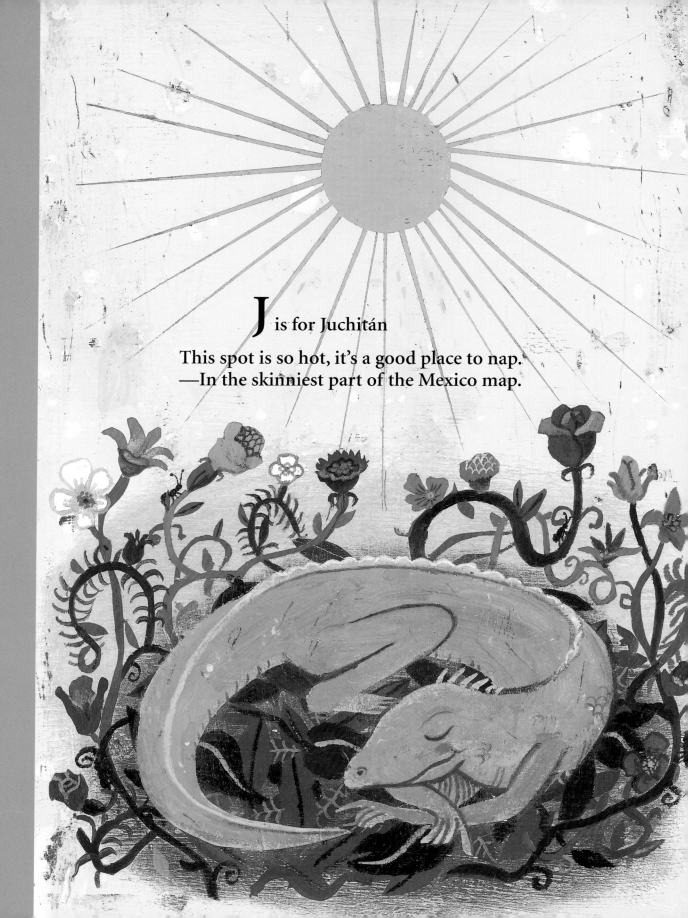

J j

J is for Juchitán

This spot is so hot, it's a good place to nap.
—In the skinniest part of the Mexico map.

Juchitán is a town on the Isthmus of Tehuantepec, a steamy and hot part of Mexico. It is a matriarchy. That is, it is run by *Juchitecas*, the local women. They are known for the beautiful traditional costumes and—no surprise!—for their strong character. And it is the birthplace of the great Mexican painter Francisco Toledo.

Because it is a tropical place, iguanas thrive around Juchitán. A marvelous photograph called "Nuestra Señora de las Iguanas" (Our Lady of the Iguanas) by Graciela Iturbide celebrates a local woman—with so many *live* iguanas perched on her head, it's hard to count them!

Both men and women from Juchitán can often be seen walking along the roads, bearing iguanas—like lizard-crowns. Since pre-Cortés times, the iguana has been a favorite food here; maybe these people will eat the iguanas when they get home.

K k

Frida Kahlo was one of the greatest Mexican painters of the twentieth century. She married another great one, Diego Rivera. Kahlo was born in 1907, but chose 1910 as her birth year instead, the start of the Mexican Revolution.

As a child she was stricken with polio, a disease that affected her legs. At age eighteen, a streetcar accident nearly killed her, and ever after she was in pain. While Kahlo was recovering, her mother rigged an apparatus so that she could paint in bed. Using a mirror, she began painting self-portraits, something she did all her life. These images show her suffering. They show her unique way of seeing things. They also show her amazing eyebrows.

Frida Kahlo loved drama. She wore flamboyant get-ups to glorify Mexico's Indian past. A favorite outfit was of a *tehuana* (a woman from Tehuantepec), with its gorgeous lacy headdress. The finishing touch to any costume was jewelry. Kahlo did not just *wear* ancient bracelets and necklaces, she was *adorned* with them. You can see these things at the Casa Azul in Mexico City.

Frida Kahlo left a legacy of photographs and paintings, each created with her revolutionary vision. Perhaps the greatest gift to us was her ferocious independence. And so many images of her famous eyebrows!

K is for Kahlo

Kahlo was a painter
who loved her Mexico.
She dressed in dashing costumes
so everyone would know.

L is for Lava

Ash, steam, molten fire
explode over the land. A
volcano is born.

Lava is red-hot rock that spurts or flows from volcanoes. You can find it (cooled down) all over Mexico because Mexico is on the Ring of Fire, the land-rim around the Pacific Ocean, where many volcanoes burst forth. The countryside is pocked with large lava mountains and cinder cones. Lava makes a great building material, except scorpions like to live in it.

Some of Mexico's most famous volcanoes are: Ixtaccíhuatl, the Ixta, or Sleeping Woman; Popocatépetl, the Popo; and Orizaba, which mountaineers from around the world try to climb each year. These days the Popo is restless. Every now and then it spews ashes. After one of Popo's "belches," ash-covered streets and cars look like they're snow-dusted.

On February 20, 1943, in the state of Michoacán, a man named Dionisio Pulido "plowed up" a volcano in his cornfield! He was working in the *milpa* when lava burbled out of the ground. Soon there stood a full-fledged volcano, the Paricutín. This was the second time ever that anyone had seen a volcano being born! It grew quickly and swallowed not only Señor Pulido's cornfield, but also several villages. Some nicknamed Paricutín "the Michoacán belch." The spectacle of a volcano spewing fire and lava was so thrilling, tourists from all over came dashing to watch the fireworks. Señor Pulido joked with visitors that his livelihood had gone up in smoke.

Ll

Maize is corn. The Mexicans call themselves the People of Corn, for they have lived on maize, *maíz*, for as long as anybody remembers. Legend says that maize was the gift to man from the god Quetzalcóatl, the plumed serpent. Maize is painted on Mexican pottery from earliest times. In ancient days it was revered and addressed as "Your Lordship."

Maize is an old, old plant. It was first domesticated in Mexico and later grown throughout the world. In the last century, some ancient corncobs were found in a cave in Mexico. The ears were tiny—about an inch (2.5 cm) or less long! And they were at least 5,000 years old!

Near Oaxaca City there is a restaurant that serves only corn—from drinks to main dishes to sweets, served with MOUNTAINS of *corn* tortillas. A poster declares: *Sin maíz no hay país* (without maize there is no country).

Corn is still sacred. It feeds the Mexican people. In some parts of Mexico, to this day, people address the corn plant as "Your Lordship."

M is for Maize

Maize is eaten many ways,
like *sopes* and *quesadillas*.
One perfect way of eating it
is humble, warm tortillas.

N is for Netzahualcóyotl

There was a golden time
once
when men lived dreams
and poems bloomed like
flowers.

N n

Netzahualcóyotl, Fasting Coyote, was a poet, lawmaker, engineer, and humanitarian. In the 1400s he ruled Texcoco. His kingdom was a famous place of learning, known by some as the Athens of the Western World.

Because of heavy summer rains, Lake Texcoco flooded each year, causing terrible problems. Netzahualcóyotl figured out how to drain the water and devised a canal system to help agriculture.

One of his great concerns was the well-being of his people. He took care of the needy, often with his own money. And he gave prizes for the best in artwork, music, and poetry; and formed a library. He designed gardens and built baths, cut from living rock, which you can still visit.

Like Leonardo da Vinci, this thinker-king was a "Renaissance Man." Some poets of his time were called *tlamatini*, meaning wise man and master of the word. Of these, Netzahualcóyotl was greatest. Only a few of his poems survived. Luckily, we still have this one:

I love the song of the mockingbird,
Bird of four hundred voices,
I love the color of the jadestone
And enervating the perfume of flowers,
But more than all I love my brother: man.

In 1968 Mexico hosted the summer Olympic Games. Athletes and visitors from around the world gathered in Mexico City, which became one big fiesta. Huge, colorful statues adorned the *anillo periférico* (freeway-ring around the city). Each statue was designed by a different country. The Mexico Olympics saw the birth of the "Fosbury flop," a new way of high jumping that is "normal" today. Many world records, such as the high jump and the long jump, were broken here. And not by a little—but a LOT.

The motto of the Mexico Olympics was: *Todo es posible en la paz* (everything is possible in peace). Doves, symbols of peace, were seen on posters, shopping bags, balloons. To begin the Games, a great flock of doves was released.

Unfortunately, before the Games, a student demonstration and its bloody result marred the event. But even so there was a strong feeling of camaraderie. In Mexico the world gathered—united for sport; united for peace.

Todo es posible en la paz. Everything is possible in peace.

O is for Olympic Games

The world went to Mexico,
held hands in brotherhood,
and for one shining moment
knew peace.

The prickly pear cactus, or *nopal*, appears on the Mexican flag. According to legend, when the *Mexica*, a tribe seeking a new home, saw an eagle clutching a snake, perched on a prickly pear cactus, they should stop. The stopping place turned out to be an island in Lake Texcoco. There they built their city, the grand Tenochtitlán (Place of the Cactus on the Stone), now Mexico City.

The prickly pear was not only a sign to settle, it was (and is) an important food. Just remove the spines, slice up a pad, and steam. The vegetable tastes a lot like green beans. The *tuna*, prickly pear fruit, is sweet and tasty. It is often sold as cactus candy.

Prickly pear plays host to cochineal, an insect that, when dried and crushed, makes a magnificent red dye. For centuries, Mexican Indians had used cochineal to color cloth. European reds were not as rich and faded easily. In 1519 when the Spanish invaded what is now Mexico, they took the cochineal from the Indians. It became their number one export, worth a fortune because the Old World was desperate for color. For 300 years other countries tried everything—from spies to piracy—to learn the secret ingredient. Cochineal may be the only bug in the world that was spied on, smuggled, and captured by pirates!

P is for Prickly Pear

All over the land
the prickly pear hold up their arms
and pray for rain.

The quetzal is a magnificent bird that lives in the towering trees of the cloud forests of Mexico and Central America. Its full name, "resplendent quetzal," describes it perfectly, for the iridescent feathers shine brilliantly. The "trail" feathers of the male grow up to three feet long, so, swooping through the jungles, he looks like a green comet.

The word "quetzal" means plume or feather in Nahuatl, the Aztec language. According to his name, Quetzalcóatl, the Feathered Serpent god of old, had plumage of quetzal feathers. In ancient times quetzal feathers were more precious than gold or jade. They were given to honor royalty. The Aztec emperor wore a headdress of quetzal plumes. The feathers were taken by trapping the birds, then releasing them to grow new ones. The punishment for killing a quetzal was death.

Maya and Aztec tales say that the quetzal must be free or it will die. Today it is dying out because of something else: logging, farming, and cattle raising are shrinking its habitat. It is so rare to see one, this secretive bird had become almost a legend. Not long ago a villager, with great awe and excitement, asked a photographer seeking the resplendent quetzal, "You've seen one? They're still alive?"

Q is for Quetzal

Quetzal, quetzal, where are you hiding?
The answer, friend, I'm not confiding.

R r

R is for Rain God

The rain god has a lot of different names,
but what he does has always been the same.
He sits up in his cloudy-damp domain
and when he wants to, lets fall all the rain.

The rain god had several names in early Mexico. To the Aztecs he was Tláloc. To the Zapotecs, Cocijo. To the Totonacs, Tajín. To the Mayas, Chaac.

But no matter what his name, people prayed to him for rain. For without rain there would be no pumpkins, no beans, no corn—no crops.

A gigantic statue of Tláloc had been "sleeping for centuries in a dry stream bed" in the little village of Coatlinchán (Home of the Snake). When the National Museum of Anthropology was being built, planners decided to place the huge Tláloc at the entrance. Hundreds of workers and engineers swarmed to the village, hoisted the giant statue onto a specially built trailer and trundled it off. In exchange, Coatlinchán got a road, a medical center, a school, and electricity.

The great Tláloc reached his new home in Mexico City on a night in April, 1964. He was greeted by 25,000 people, thronging the streets. The "welcoming committee" was greeted with the worst downpour ever for that normally dry season! And it has been raining more than usual in Mexico City ever since.

No matter what his name, people still believe in the rain god.

Skeletons, *calacas*, are seen everywhere in Mexico. Every day. You see them in folk art: bands of clay skeleton musicians, skeleton card players, and skeletons crowded onto buses. There are skeleton earrings. Skeleton magnets. Skeleton mouse pads. Skeleton postcards. Skeleton piñatas. Skeletons strung with firecrackers. Skeleton mugs for drinking punch. There are people dressed as skeletons in plays and dances. And a mural by Diego Rivera shows Mexican society people dressed in their finery, ambling through Alameda Park. The main figure is a be-plumed skeleton wearing a feather boa.

Apart from Mother's Day, The Day of the Dead, *El día de los muertos*, is the biggest holiday in Mexico. Actually, it spans three days, from October 31 to November 2, and it is the time to remember those who are gone. That time of year there are more skeletons around than ever. Sugar skulls decorate people's houses. A famous bakery fills its sweets cases with cookies shaped like skeleton bones; and skeleton puppets slide down wires from the ceiling to the floor, shrieking the while.

Skeletons abound because Mexicans do not hide from death. They know it is closely connected to life.

S is for Skeleton

Skeleton, skeleton, why do you dance?
I love to move. I love to prance—
sometimes with partners; sometimes alone—
to show off my rackety, clackety bones.

T is for Tomb

The king slept long, under tons of rubble
Till Ruz came digging with his shovel.

The tomb of the Maya king Pakal (Shield) was found in 1949 at Palenque, an ancient Maya place. The archeologist, Alberto Ruz, discovered the grave when he noticed a double row of stone-plugged holes in one slab in the floor of the Temple of the Inscriptions.

It took four digging seasons to remove tons of rubble that had been flung into the hidden staircase to keep grave robbers away. On June 15, 1952, searchers at last opened the crypt and looked upon an immense stone sarcophagus not seen since 683, when the king was buried. Pakal became king at age 12; he died at age 80. When the five-ton (4535 kg), gorgeously carved lid was lifted, the men gazed at the royal bones, encrusted with a jade mask (340 separate pieces!); jade bracelets; a jade necklace; a jade crown; a jade ring on every finger; a jade bead in the mouth. Jade, jade, JADE, apple-green—to the Maya, the most precious of riches.

The tomb is closed to visitors. So, if you visit the replica in Mexico City, close your eyes; pretend you are in the steamy jungle at Palenque. The temple steps are *very* narrow. And slimy because of endless rain that seeps in. It is dark. And dank. And there is no rail to grab on to. Listen to the howler monkeys in the trees, screaming like jaguars. Imagine you are an olden Maya. Now, enter the tomb.

The Usumacinta, one of Mexico's great rivers, flows into the Gulf of Mexico. It creates a natural border between Mexico and Guatemala, where cacao, the "chocolate plant," once grew wild. In ancient times it was an important waterway for trade; barges still carry goods along it.

Where it snakes its way past Yaxchilán, an ancient Maya city, the river is nearly 650 feet (198 m) wide! The Usumacinta is so powerful and so scornful of the puny works of man, over the centuries it has gobbled up several majestic monuments built along its banks.

U
u

U is for Usumacinta River

The Usumacinta River
is a very long wet shiver
of shimmering water—a quiver—
sometimes wide; sometimes a sliver.

The vaquero is the Mexican cowboy, the original. His history began with the great horsemen of Arabia, and the traditions came to Mexico with the Spaniards. The word "vaquero" comes from "*vaca*," cow in Spanish, and means a person who looks after and knows his way around cattle.

The life of the vaquero was a hard one. His day began at two or three in the morning, until pitch dark—or all night, if the herd stampeded or some other trouble erupted. In the early days, a vaquero made his own equipment, for there were no stores selling such gear. In "off hours," he worked up spurs and conchos (buttons) of silver; and a range of rawhide equipment: hackamores (a kind of bridle), quirts (whips), reins and, of course, lariats, the rawhide ropes used to lasso ornery cow-critters. "Lariat" comes from the Spanish, *la reata*. Making one involved killing a cow and working the hide: curing, pounding, tugging, tallowing, stretching, and braiding. It took weeks to make, but the *reata* was an item of beauty. It did the job and was worth the work.

The true vaqueros are nearly gone. But some still remain, clinging to a life, hard but independent. Today, for any cowboy, or cowgirl, to be dubbed "vaquero" is the ultimate compliment.

V is for Vaquero

Of all the cowboys, he's the king.
With lariat and piggin' string,
he can do most anything.

W is for Weave

The woman kneels at her backstrap loom,
weaving fabric sun to sun.
The pattern worked into the yarn,
tells you where the wearer's from.

Weaving is done in many Mexican villages. But once, all clothing and other articles for daily use were woven at home or by local weavers. Each village, *pueblo*, had its own particular weaving traditions; people near and far knew your homeplace by what you wore—the *faja*, sash; the *camisa*, shirt; the *huipil*, woman's dress-like garment. You could spot the head man, *mandón*, of a village by the *faja* alone. One Amusgo Indian *huipil* is unmistakable. It is woven from naturally brown cotton called *coyuche*, coyote-colored.

The weaving is done with a backstrap loom, usually by women. One end of the loom is looped around a fixed object, like a tree; the other, around the weaver's waist. The weaver works kneeling, often on a *petate*, a woven mat.

Patterns have been passed down for centuries from weaver to weaver. Where Huichol Indians live, it is said that the Huichol man captures a rattlesnake and brings it to his wife; she then closes her eyes and moves her hands slowly above the snake. When she weaves a faja, the pattern appears—a bold design resembling the back of a rattlesnake.

W
W

Xochimilco means "place where the flowers grow." The village sprouted on the shores of one of five ancient lakes in the Valley of Mexico. Of those, only a few puddles remain of Lake Texcoco and Lake Xochimilco.

This was a squishy little place, where long-ago people used *chinampas* to grow flowers and vegetables. *Chinampas*, floating gardens, were enormous baskets filled with lake sludge, so rich it could grow just about any-thing. When plants from the baskets rooted in the lake bottom, the chinampas became permanent. Chinampas were also ridged fields, where ditches were dug to drain off lake water.

Xochimilco is still a place where flowers grow. You can glide the garden-lined canals in a flower-bedecked canoe, with a name like Rosa or Dolores, and enjoy the "floating gardens."

X is for Xochimilco

Along old waterways
flowers opening. Oh smell
the fragrant blossoms!

The yoke, *yugo*, was a piece of equipment used in an ancient ball game, probably first played on the Gulf coast, the land of the "rubber people." Maybe made of leather, it fitted around a player's waist like a wide belt and was used as protection from the hard, solid rubber ball.

Ball courts have been uncovered all over Mexico. Some still have stone rings along the walls. Spectators came bedecked in their best "bling" to root their team on. If the ball got through one of the rings, winners were allowed to grab the spectators' jewels. So the public fled, with the victors hot on their heels.

Nobody knows exactly how it was played, but we get clues from early pottery, statues, and writings from Cortés's time. It seems that the ball had to be always in motion. At first, people played using hips, knees, elbows only. Later it was okay to use hands and feet. Whatever archeologists learn, two things are certain: it was rough and the stakes were high. When the game was over, sometimes the losers, sometimes the *winners,* lost their lives!

U-shaped yokes of stone grace art collections and museums. These are copies of the leather yokes and were never worn. They are elaborately carved in shapes of frogs, stylized clouds, owls with delicate feathers, or absolutely plain and smooth—all made without metal tools! They are some of the finest sculptures of the Americas.

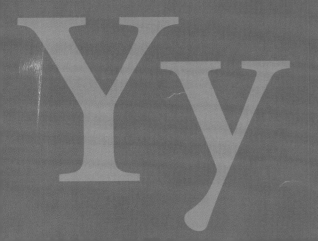

Yy

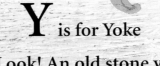

Y is for Yoke

Look! An old stone yoke
made two thousand years ago by
someone who knew beauty!

111111001001
0100010010001
0001110010 01
0100 10 10 10 10
1 00100 10001001
1100 11111111100
111 111 0010 0
0100 010 01000
0111 0010 010

O

Z is for Zero

The state of numbers was very grave.
Nobody could think up zero
until an Olmec's great brainwave.
Mexico's the zero-hero!

Zero may seem like nothing, but it's really SOMETHING!

In Mexico the Olmecs were the first people in the world to think of zero, centuries before it was "invented" in India. Europeans never did hit upon zero by themselves; they learned from other people.

The idea of zero is the basis for our mathematics. It shows that a certain place shouldn't be counted. It is also a "place holder." Using "nothing," early Mexicans devised a way of numbering by position. We count from left to right; ancient Mexicans counted from bottom to top. Their system was based on groups of twenties. Ours, the decimal system, is based on counting our (ten) fingers. The Mexicans used both fingers and toes, what the Maya called "the whole man."

The idea of zero is one of the greatest achievements of man's mind. And the Mexicans came up with it! Zow! They don't get a zero, they get 1,000,000,000,000 gold stars!

Tony Johnston

Tony Johnston has written many acclaimed books for young people. She and her husband lived in Mexico for fifteen years, where they raised their children. Mexico has inspired much of her work, including *Day of the Dead, The Tale of Rabbit and Coyote, Angel City, My Mexico, The Ancestors Are Singing*, and *Any Small Goodness: A Novel of the Barrio*. Mrs. Johnston lives in Southern California.

John Parra

John Parra grew up in Southern California, enriched in Hispanic roots. This cultural knowledge inspires his award-winning artwork, which has been showcased in galleries throughout the U.S. John received the International Latino Book Award for his illustration work on his first children's book, *My Name is Gabriela*. He believes that "there is a natural passion for art that begins early in our lives, that the instinct to create is in us all, and with art serving as a divine state of both imagination and reality, we are able to express the inexpressible." John lives in New York City.